Leonardo Da Vinci's Role in the Renaissance

Children's Renaissance History

BABY PROFESSOR

EDUCATION KIDS

Leonardo da Vinci is most remembered as an artist. But he was also an architect, chronicler of science, and an inventor.

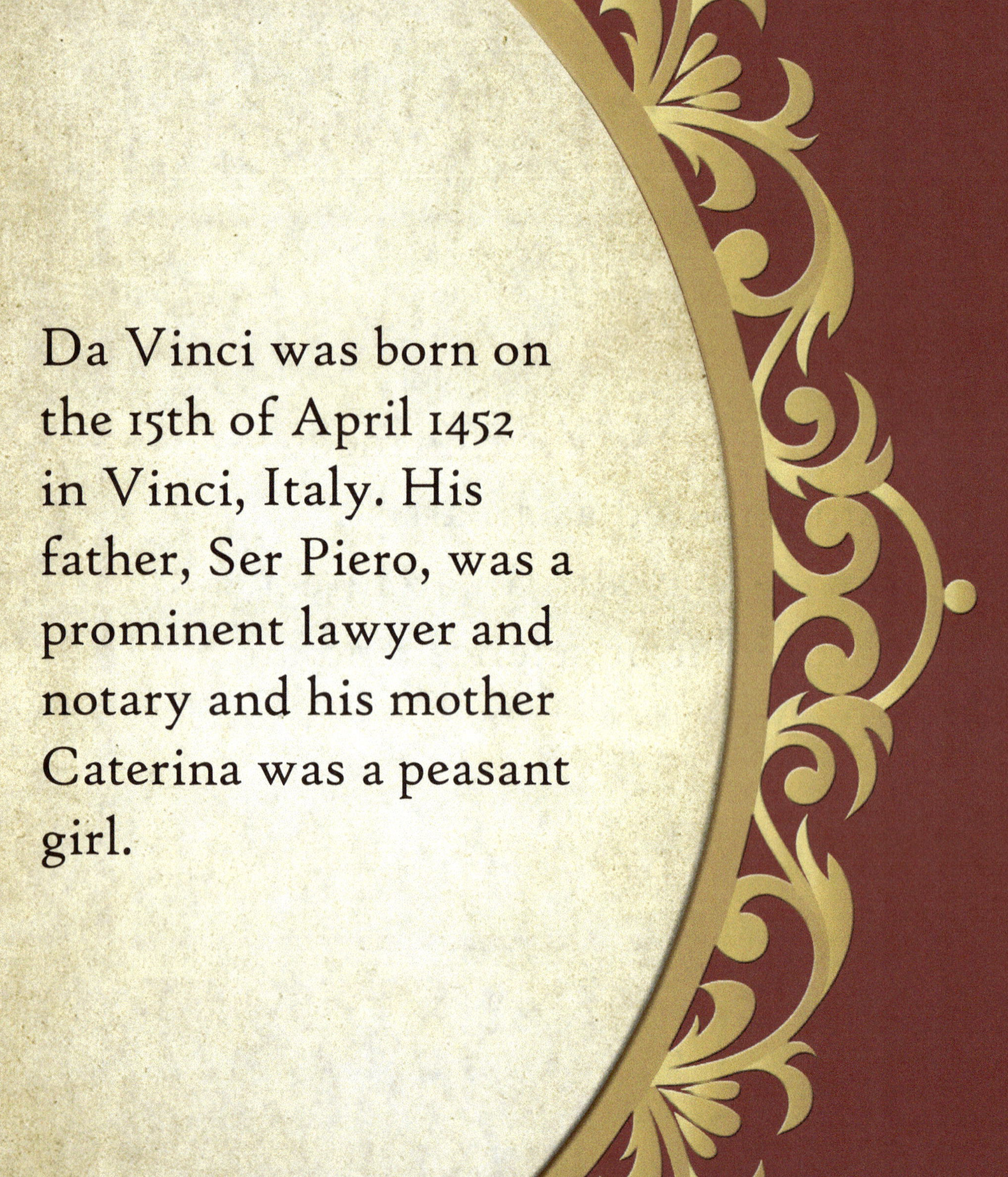

Da Vinci was born on the 15th of April 1452 in Vinci, Italy. His father, Ser Piero, was a prominent lawyer and notary and his mother Caterina was a peasant girl.

Since Leonardo's parents were not married, he was raised by Ser Piero with several stepmothers.

He lived his early years on his father's family estate in Vinci. During this period, an uncle influenced him to love nature.

Da Vinci did not receive much
of a formal education beyond
basic reading, writing and
mathematical skills.

When he was 14 or 15, Ser Piero sent him to apprentice with Andrea del Verrocchio, a sculptor and painter in Florence.

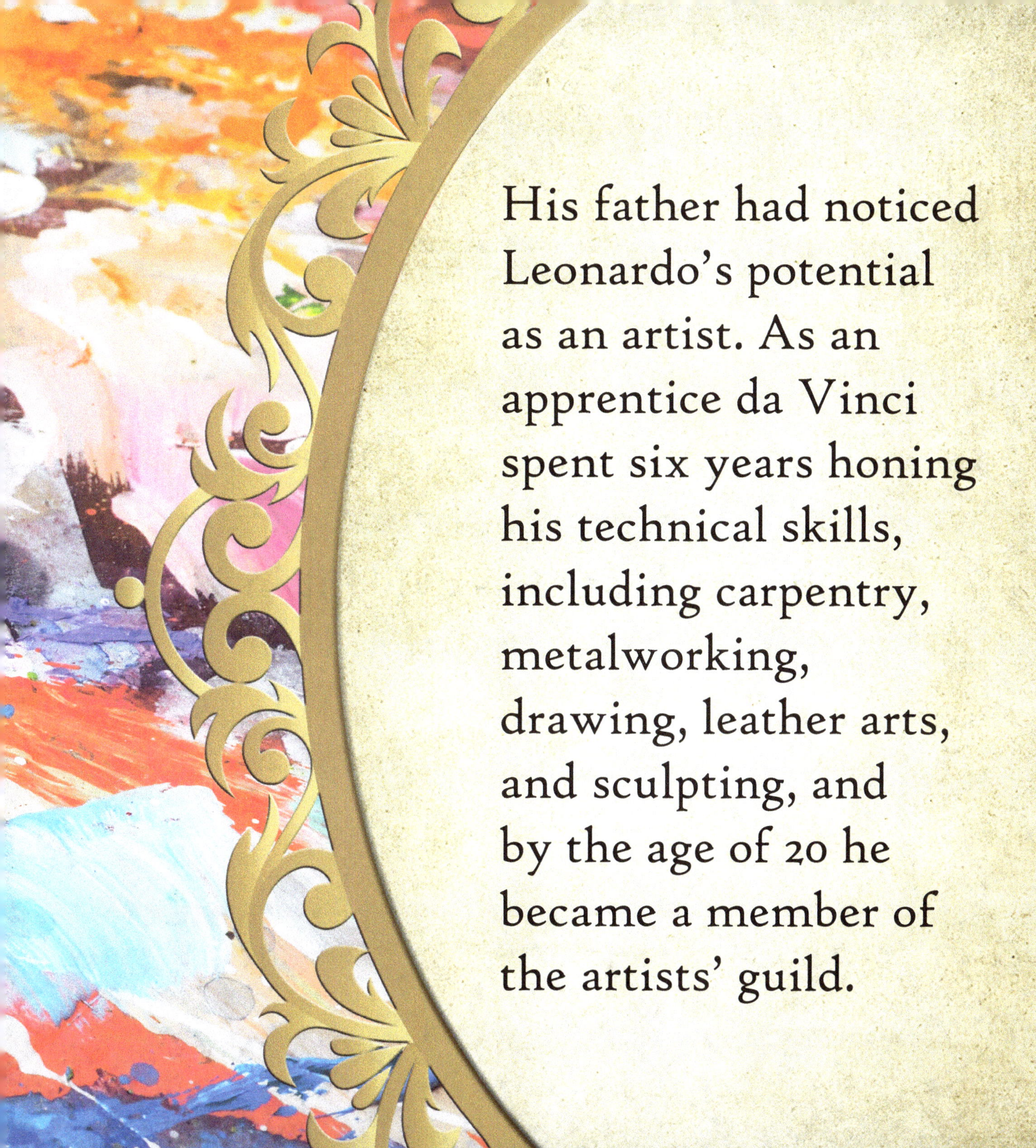

His father had noticed
Leonardo's potential
as an artist. As an
apprentice da Vinci
spent six years honing
his technical skills,
including carpentry,
metalworking,
drawing, leather arts,
and sculpting, and
by the age of 20 he
became a member of
the artists' guild.

The apprentices contributed
to del Verrocchio's works, and
Leonardo's style is evident in
paintings from the studio by
1475.

He stayed with Verrocchio
until he became an independent
master in 1478. At that time,
he took The Adoration of the
Magi as his first commissioned
work for Florence's San Donato
monastery.

He never finished this
work, since he was soon
lured to Milan to serve
as an architect, engineer,
sculptor, and painter
for the ruling Sforza
dynasty.

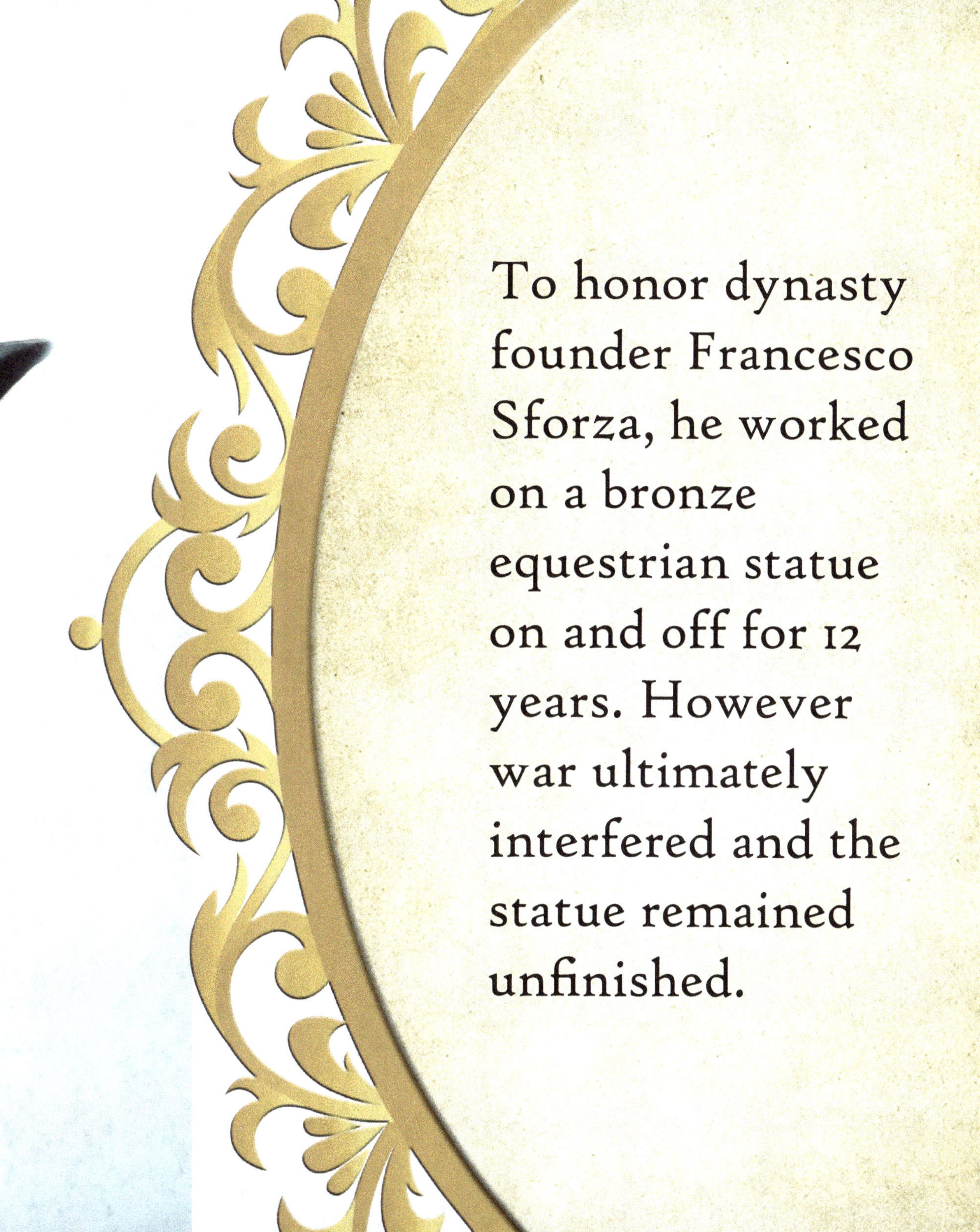

To honor dynasty founder Francesco Sforza, he worked on a bronze equestrian statue on and off for 12 years. However war ultimately interfered and the statue remained unfinished.

As a man of Renaissance

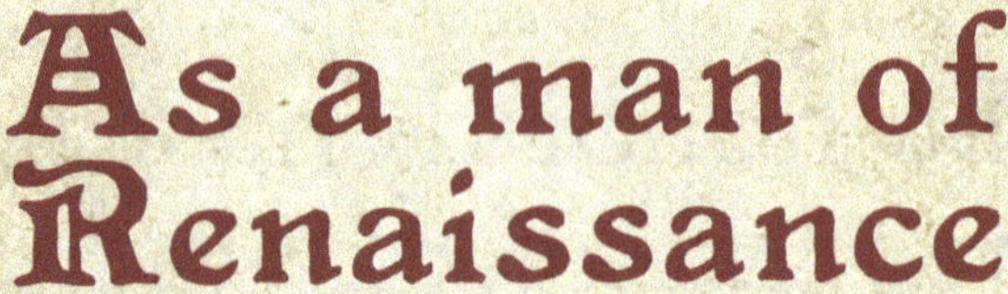

Due to the war, da Vinci did not complete many of his paintings and other works. Because of his diverse interests that included the laws of science and the study of and nature, he was often sidetracked.

In the early 1490s, he began
writing down his thoughts
on human anatomy, painting,
mechanics, and architecture.

His notebooks contained wide-ranging ideas, which include plans for a bicycle, a flying machine, and drawings of the human skeleton and even an unborn baby.

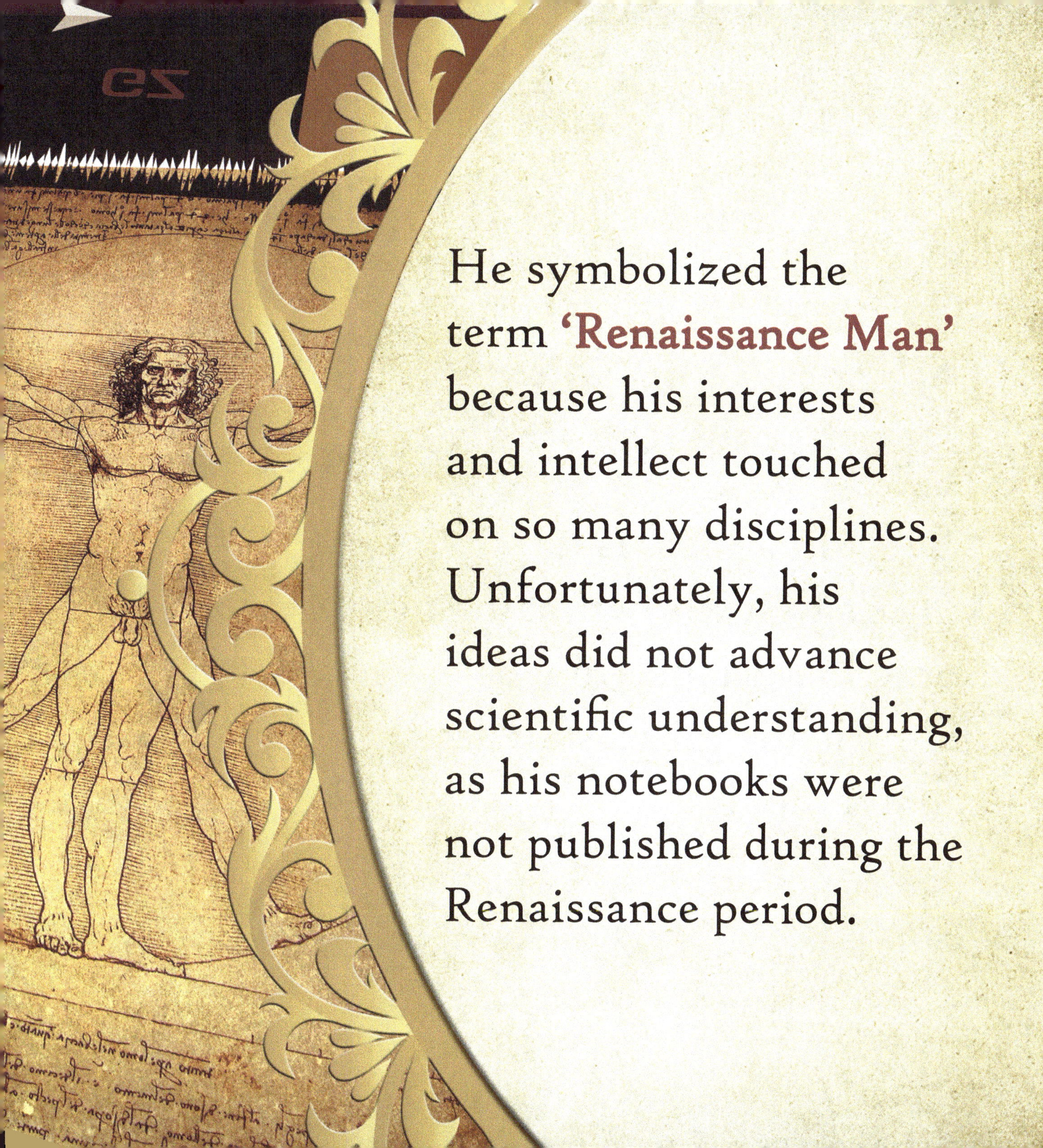

He symbolized the term **'Renaissance Man'** because his interests and intellect touched on so many disciplines. Unfortunately, his ideas did not advance scientific understanding, as his notebooks were not published during the Renaissance period.

Greatest works of Leonardo da Vinci

The **'Mona Lisa'** is da Vinci's best-known painting. Some historians argued that it is his greatest artistic achievement.

Art historians have identified
Lisa del Giocondo as the subject.
She is the wife of a wealthy
silk merchant, Francesco del
Giocondo.

Historians believed that the painting was commissioned for the Giocondos' home to commemorate the birth of their second child.

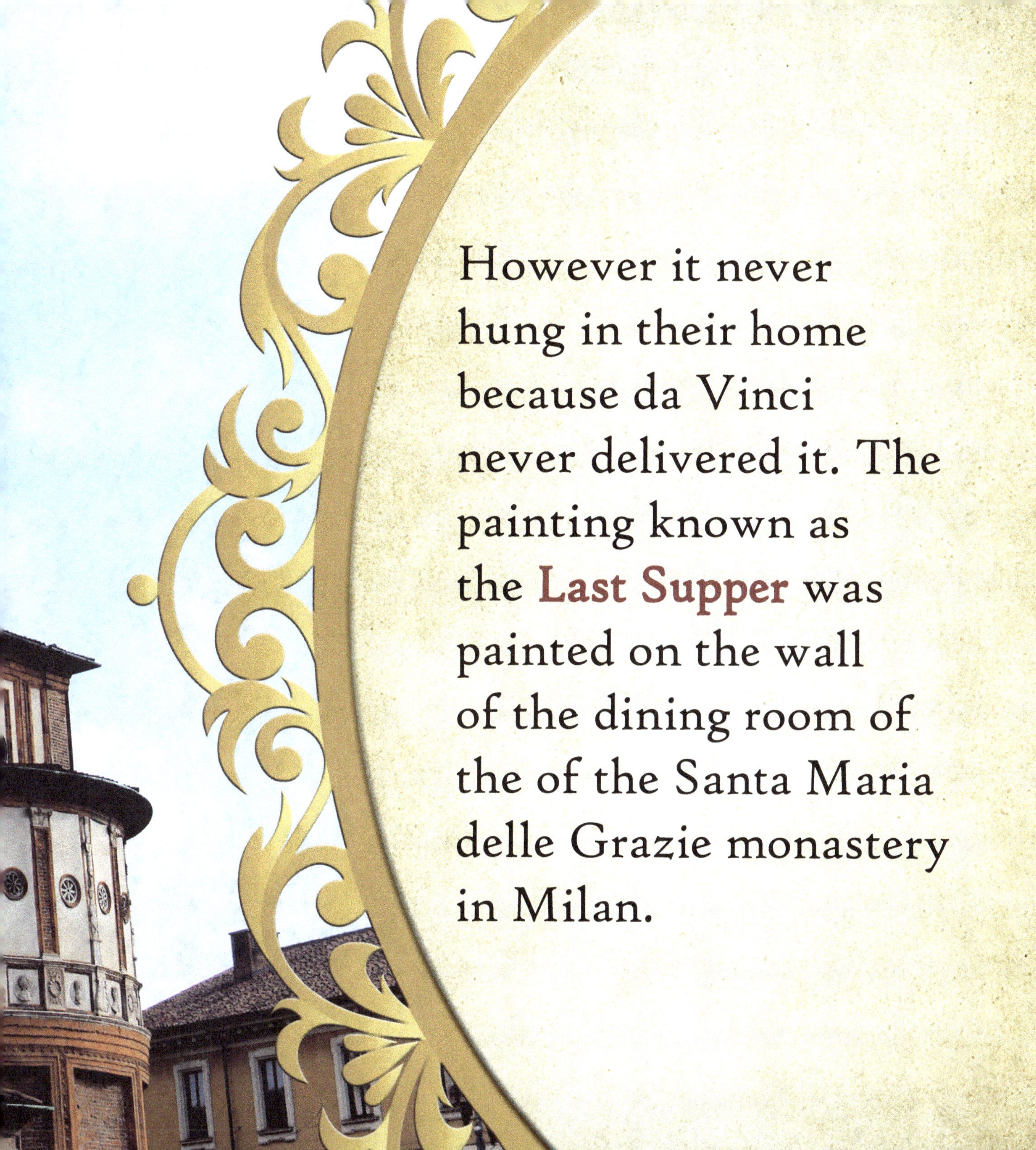

However it never hung in their home because da Vinci never delivered it. The painting known as the **Last Supper** was painted on the wall of the dining room of the of the Santa Maria delle Grazie monastery in Milan.

It shows the scene
when Jesus told His
apostles that one of
them would soon
betray him. He worked
on this from 1492 to
1498.

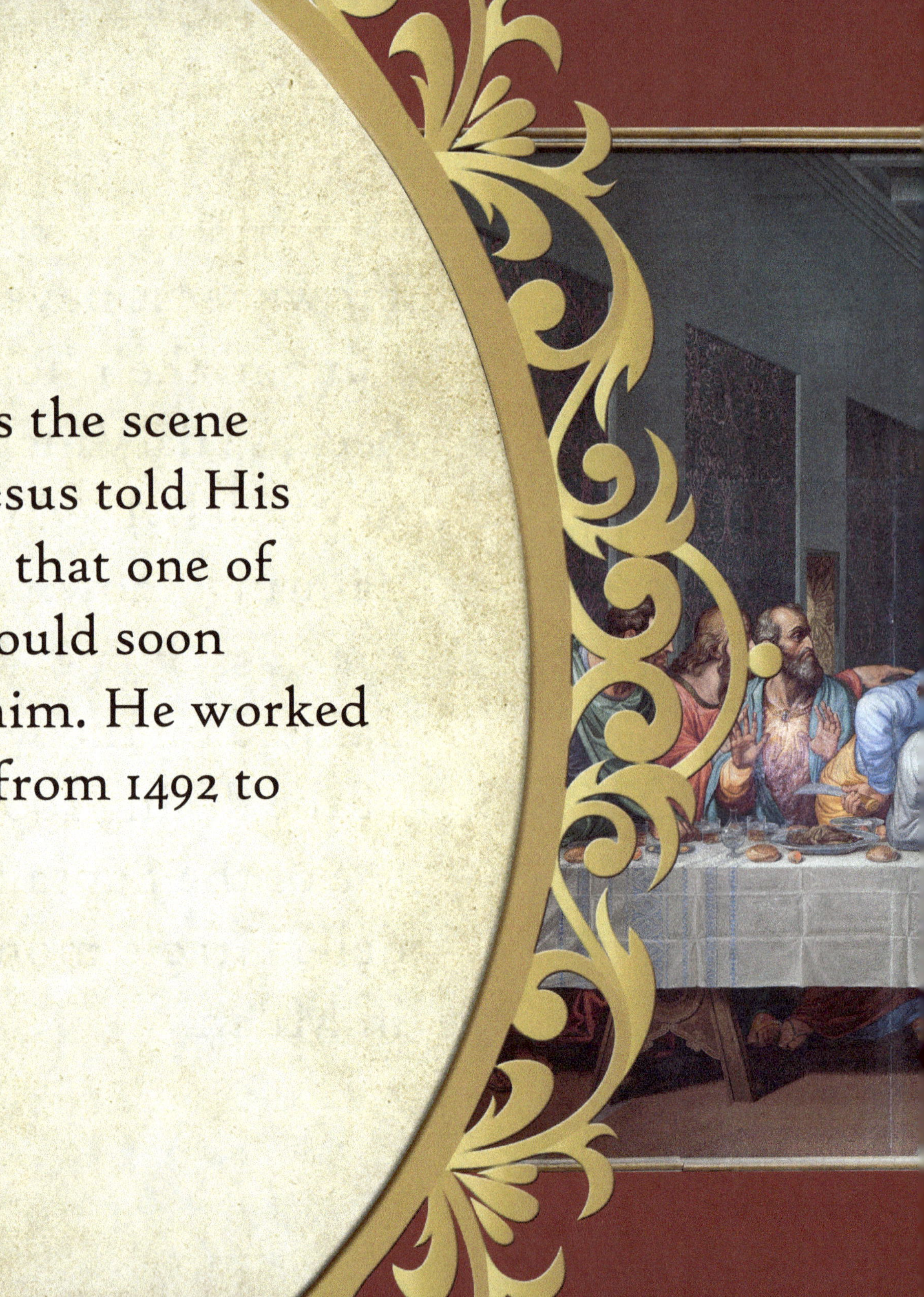

It was not done with the traditional fresco technique. Da Vinci chose to try to paint on the wall in layers. Because of this, the masterpiece deteriorated during his lifetime.

It has undergone an extensive restoration in recent years to preserve it. When he was 60, da Vinci made a self-portrait known as 'Portrait of a man in red chalk'.

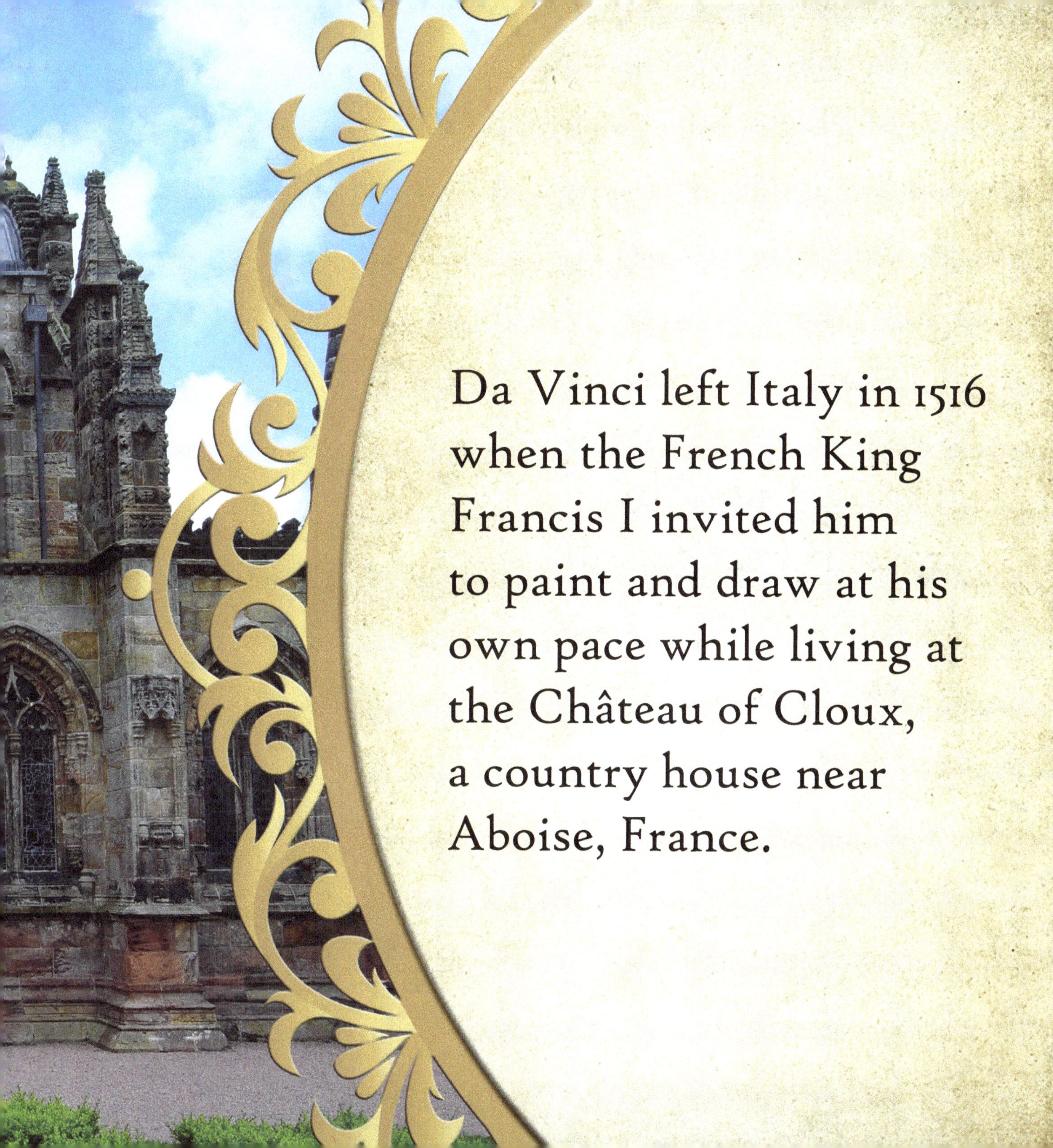

Da Vinci left Italy in 1516 when the French King Francis I invited him to paint and draw at his own pace while living at the Château of Cloux, a country house near Aboise, France.

He spent just three
years in France and
died there on the 2nd
of May 1519.

Visit
BABY PROFESSOR
EDUCATION KIDS
www.BabyProfessorBooks.com
to download Free Baby Professor eBooks
and view our catalog of new and exciting
Children's Books